All Scripture references taken from the KJV of the Holy Bible, unless otherwise indicated.

Break Free from Collective Captivity

by Dr. Marlene Miles

Freshwater Press 2024

ISBN: 978-1-963164-27-5

Paperback Version

Copyright 2024, Dr. Marlene Miles

All rights reserved. No part of this book may be reproduced, distributed or transmitted by any means or in any means including photocopying, recording or other electronic or mechanical methods without prior written permission of the publisher except in the case of brief publications or critical reviews.

Table of Contents

Break Free From

COLLECTIVE

CAPTIVITY

Freshwater

Psalm 126

When the LORD turned again the captivity of Zion, we were like them that dream.

Then was our mouth filled with laughter, and our tongue with singing: then said they among the heathen, The LORD hath done great things for them.

The LORD hath done great things for us; *whereof* we are glad.

Turn again our captivity, O LORD, as the streams in the south.

They that sow in tears shall reap in joy.

He that goeth forth and weepeth, bearing precious seed, shall doubtless come again with rejoicing, bringing his sheaves *with him.*

Group Pressure

Group pressure and peer pressure is real. There is also such a thing as mob mentality. If one person in a group does something others are likely to also do it. Life is spiritual, people are spiritual and that's why many times what drives people to do what others are doing is *spiritual*. When your mother said if Bobby jumped off a bridge would you jump too? Sad news is whatever *spirit* is influencing Bobby might also be influencing you especially if you and Bobby are related by blood, or even if you're not related, but you two *run* together, or have made covenants, soul ties, or vows to one another.

A family is a group. Whether that family is in the same house or not is not material, if that family has the same blood coursing through their veins, they are a family and are subject to similar things happening either <u>to</u> them or *for* them in their lives.

Some people are naturally loners, most are not; it's about a 30/70 split. Some folks are not happy unless they are socializing or in a group or with a bunch of people.

What family were you born into? Where were you born? What city, country, what continent? It all makes a difference. I'm not trying to make anyone who doesn't know exactly where and *who* they are from, such as an adopted person, or someone born of a surrogate feel bad, or any type of way. I especially am not doing that because I don't exactly know what country my ancestors were from originally. I know what continents, but not the exact countries. By 23 & Me and other genetic testing I've pinpointed the general area, but I have at least one sister who will argue with me on that.

I once asked a grown man about his grandparents and he said that he didn't know them, never met them, and asked me, *What difference does it make?* He also admitted that after he left home as a young adult it never occurred to him to call home periodically to check on his parents. Of course, he is a man who knows nothing about himself and is totally unspiritual. He's wrong, because it does make a difference where you come from and who your people are. How will you do spiritual mapping in your family if you don't even know anything about your family?

What Are You *Attached* To?

Where do you live?

Unless you are fully in Christ then you are subject to the territorial *spirits* of the area/region where you live. However, no matter where you live, if you are fully in Christ, then you can walk any place and among any people – and the devil will not be able to touch you. Jesus said, **The prince of this world cometh, and he has nothing in me**. When you **are** Christ, or you are fully *in* Christ, then you can also say that the devil has nothing in you.

Jesus slipped through crowds and evaded mobs of people that wanted to kill Him. How did He do that? Jesus was *in* the world but not *of* it. To me being *of* a thing means attached to it in some human way, physically, or emotionally, for example.

Situations where others would have been caught or trapped did not ensnare Jesus. He was different and His situation was different.

There may be situations where you, yourself, may not be seen, but what you are **stuck to** or attached to is so large or so obvious that it makes you **seen** – whether you want to be seen, or not.

Think of some of the movies you've watched where someone is trying to get away from a pursuer, but they stop in the middle of the attempted get away to talk to, embrace, or interact with another person as if time has stopped. Time hasn't stopped. Neither has the pursuer, but the person who was trying to escape was so tied to something or someone in the world that they stopped to meet them, greet them, hug them, explain something to them and by doing so, it completely slowed them down. Now, they are caught. That person was *tied* to the world rather than wearing it loosely, and that attachment caused them to get caught.

You need to be different, and your situations need to be different in the same way Jesus was. The most assured way to do that is to be fully in Christ.

Who are your people?

While it might seem judgey to need to know who one's people are, it is important to search this out. What race were you born into? What culture? It matters. No one can say it doesn't matter, because it does.

Even if you think you are an absolute loner, you are part of a collective. That collective will either be <u>in</u> the world and ***of*** the world, unless you are 100% in Christ. As a matter of fact, you may be part of more than one collective in this physical world, at the same time. Being in a collective or a group, you share in the glory, or the shame of that organization. Well, that is, when we are **OF** the world. The only way not to be of the world is to be **<u>completely</u>** in Christ.

Some years ago, an ensemble of popular voices sang a song, ***We Are the World****,* because they are, and they *were* the world, and they were singing to the *world*. That is not the aspiration for a Christian, however. We are <u>in</u> the world, but not *of* it. To want to be in both places, in the Kingdom of God and also in the world at the same time is untenable and it is dangerous and displeasing to God. Actually, it is displeasing to the spirit world – both sides of it.

Jesus walked **on** water. How did He do that? Jesus was **in** this world, this Earth realm, but not *of* it. Jesus walked by and was **in** the Spirit.

Well, we are supposed to be in this world, but not *of* it. People who are *of* the world are subject <u>to</u> the world. People who are *of* the world are subject to the elements of this world. People *of* the world are **in** the world because they are predominantly **in** their flesh. Spirit can be *in* this world and not *of* it, not mixing with it and not getting entangled with it. Don't get me wrong, spirit can get entangled with spirit, just as flesh gets entangled with flesh, but we are not talking about that right now.

Flesh is *of* the world while being **in** it— 24/7. Flesh can't walk on water, but spirit can. Flesh is 70% water and needs water, uses water, so as long as water has authority over flesh, when flesh approaches water, water will envelope it. Spirit can graze over any physical element of this world…and not be affected by it. Spirit is not water, doesn't use water and does not owe water anything, so Spirit can walk over water. Spirit has authority over water. Flesh does not.

Spirit can function and not be affected by any physical law. Flesh is subject to every physical law, gravity, centrifugal force, and et cetera.

I can ask now, instead of waiting until later on in this book, where do you live, primarily? In the Spirit, or in your flesh? If you live in and walk by the Spirit, the Word says you will not fulfill the works of the flesh. If you do not fulfill the flesh, and your ancestors didn't leave you any booby traps, then you should not ever become a captive, at least not individually. In addition, in the Spirit, you have authority over the elements of the world.

If evil overtakes a person and they denounce God and join up with Satan, they themselves can defect from the Kingdom of God, else no other witchcraft or evil can pluck them out of God's hands. Worse, if they were related to you, you now have witchcraft or occultism in your bloodline, but they are still in your family. Are you your brother's keeper? Yes, in a sense. That means that you should care that your siblings are saved, both for themselves and for the impact their spiritual status will have on the family bloodline.

Even if you form some type of a clique' or alliance with some other disgruntled siblings and agree on it like Joseph's brothers did, you can't kick them out of the family as discussed in my books, **The Robe: The Lessons of Joseph (Part One & Part Two).** Therefore, their spiritual status will affect their bloodline as they grow up, get married and have their own family. As well their spiritual status will impact the family of origin, as you all have the same blood and if raised in the same house are subject to the collective captivity of your family bloodline, if there be any.

As you can't kick anyone out of a family, because their blood still makes you relatives. You cannot kick them out of the collective, so whatever good comes to that family they have authority to partake of it. If something bad comes to that family, everyone suffers because of being in collective captivity. However, one individual can get out of collective captivity, even if the others choose to stay in it, or will not do the work to get out of it.

The only way out is through Christ Jesus.

Collective captivity starts with the family that you're born into. Collective captivity can come by the groups, clubs, societies, cults, or sects you join or associate with. The church you join up with – , even your church.

Sometimes it is the family that you marry into. Yup, you are marrying your spouse AND their whole family because you are now getting into their bloodline. And, they are mixing it up with your bloodline, as well. Wouldn't it be smart to find out what is in that bloodline that you are promising for richer and for poorer to?

You are certainly a candidate for collective captivity if you are overly attached to this world and the things of this world. If you are soul tied, you are already in captivity. If you love to keep up with the Jones', are overly social, and can't even spend a moment alone – you've just got to be in a group all the time, you are likely to fall into collective captivity, if you are not already in it from your family of origin.

If you are not all in, fully in Christ then you are in collective captivity. The many idols of this world all demand worship and when you don't acknowledge or worship them, they collect you as a captive. As said, unless you are in Christ, you can be in more than one collective at once.

Born Into It

Because of the activity of one sorcerer, the entire city of Samaria was held in captivity; so collective captivity is real. (Acts 8). Cult leaders are sorcerers. Strongmen of families are sorcerers. Household witches and warlocks are all sorcerers who hold families and groups captive, whether the family realizes it or not. Most often, they do not realize it, else they wouldn't be controlled, or controllable.

There is a woman who has at least half of her family bamboozled into thinking she's a nice person. She is a witch and those who believe her are under her spell. The rest can see who she is and are violently opposed to her bad acts within the family.

In another household, a man rules by threats and violence against his wife and family. Also, in his elderly father's and mother's house down the road from his own home, they are afraid that he will be displeased or have a tantrum, so they all walk gently on his bipolar eggshells to keep him happy. This violent man has them all in collective captivity. It is a spiritual problem, but this man is the human strongman of the family keeping the family under subjection and rule of the idols and demons of that man's house, or of that man's father's house that have found the next generation to oppress.

Every family has idols – an outside attack can only be successful against you if they can get to your family's idol... that idol is the strongman of your family.

Certain destinies are corporate. By no choice of your own, you are born into the good or the bad of a family, a neighborhood, a community, a state, a nation--, even a continent. This is why I asked you early on where you or where are your people from? It is so you will begin to consider all these things.

When what is happening to one is happening to all, it is not just a coincidence, it is collective captivity. That collective family or group may be under familial, ancestral, generational or geographical spells or curses.

Most often, people under curses do the *opposite* of what they should do and make bad decisions.

Collective captivity remains when there is unconfessed, unrepented sin. This could be your own individual sin which will not necessarily make your siblings captive—but it can. It will, however, certainly trap your generations – your kids and their kids.

If we confess our sins, he is faithful and just to forgive us our sins, and to cleanse us from all unrighteousness, (1 John 1:9).

You don't believe in God? That is sin, collective captivity is possible for groups and societies that don't believe in God, or reject God – knowingly, or unknowingly. You may be surprised at how many people take secret oaths, vows, and end up worshipping idols and not even realizing that they are doing it. Most don't believe it if you tell them. These groups, societies, et cetera are in collective captivity, no matter what they think.

Collective captivity starts and remains if you commit and continue in works of the flesh such as unforgiveness, bitterness, etc. If you do not feed on the Word of God, your spirit man will be weak, so your soul will be fodder for the devil.

Setting your hands to the plow and then turning back will lead to collective captivity. Partial deliverance will lead to collective captivity.

Having a full flesh life leads to captivity, individual and if your entire family is that way, collective captivity. If that full flesh life was lived by your ancestor – even one you don't even know, have never known, will never know – one who is long, long gone ---and that person lived in flesh addictions--- that ancestor's generations are likely to get caught and put into collective captivity.

Folks who don't believe in deliverance won't seek it out. Folks who say, *It don't take all that*, won't take all the steps to get deliverance. Folks who don't take it seriously are making matters worse for themselves and their generations as sin lingers and festers into iniquity.

Thank God for exposing the demons and trust Him to expel them completely--, take your whole deliverance, and afterwards, get filled with the

Holy Spirit so that you will be able to retain your deliverance.

Of all the works of the flesh, pride is the biggest ticket. It is one of the marks of the beast and God hates it perfectly. Pride is idolatry of self. There is vain pride and selfish pride—they are both pride.

In the Book of Revelation, judgment is pronounced on the church at Laodicea that thought it was rich and finely dressed, but that entire Church was poor, wretched and naked. Only pride pumps a man up to believe something that is totally untrue but makes him think himself glorious. The church in Laodicea doesn't exist today but since the archaeological digs are completed, you can visit the ruins of that city. Any city that Jesus pronounced woe on were cursed cities (Matthew 11:20-23 and most of the cities were destroyed.

Captivity is for the purpose of future destruction depending on what the captor either chooses to do, or is allowed to do based on the soul, heart and repentance of the person, family, or group that is captive.

Evil Dedication

Sometimes the reason all the same bad stuff happens in a family is because of evil dedication. In many non-Christian societies and in some families who believe they are Christians they go with tradition, and they may dedicate their child or children to idols thinking they are helping the child or protecting the child, but they are really transferring ownership of that child's life to an idol *god*.

The rules to that idol's ownership are peculiar to the dedication, that idol *god* and what the family believes or what the idol *god* demands.

When the parameters of that dedication is not met by the humans, the idol *gods* get enraged and begin to do bad things to that person and or family if the whole family is dedicated. The whole family can be dedicated years ago by ancestors. Even if the current parents don't dedicate the child, all these ancient dedications could be standing in a family. So, as soon as the child is born it **belongs** to that idol *god*. And, when the next child is born, same thing, and so on.

Getting out of evil dedication takes more than getting saved and born again, but it is the first step. However, getting born again and just going through the motions will bring rage out of that idol, especially if you are just playing, just trying it out, hedging your bets, or layering on Christianity with all the other idolatrous things you are doing. Folks, this is why trying to mix religions is so dangerous--, you make the idol gods mad, but if you are not fully in Christ – in enough for God to protect you, you have set up a spiritual storm that no one in their right mind would want to endure.

Playing peek-a-boo with God, coming in and out of Christianity is so dangerous. Being a Sunday Christian and a hell raiser the rest of the week – do you have a death wish? God is not mocked, and idols have no mercy.

Without a body in the Earth the devil has no power. He is therefore looking for bodies to use – even though they look alive, they are spiritually dead, being separated from God. It's why every time you try to serve God something happens either to you, or to your worship, the money you would use to worship. And, the devil is desperate to keep a body that he is using for evil in the Earth--, willing or unwilling, knowingly or unknowingly.

Dedications can involve families, towns, villages, cities and even nations, which results in collective captivity. Get out of your evil dedication as soon as you are aware of it. It's not so simple as saying so, you will have to be violent and do violent resistance and warfare.

WARFARE:

- I separate myself and my generations from the evil collective of my family of birth by the power in the Blood of Jesus.
- Slave masters of my father's house, release me and let me go, in the Name of Jesus.
- Pharaoh of my mother's house, release me and let me go, in the Name of Jesus.
- Every evil power controlling my life, lose your grip, and let me go, in the Name of Jesus.

Break Evil Dedication:

- Renounce evil dedication whether you did it or your parents, or your ancestors.
- Break and/or reverse evil dedication:
- Renounce the Dedication.
- Repent.
- Get out of the works of the flesh, especially unforgiveness. Forgive everyone.
- Ask for Mercy and to be covered with the Blood of Jesus.
- Renounce and break all evil covenants keeping the evil dedication in place.
- Break all curses associated with the evil dedication.
- Plead the Blood of Jesus to separate you from the source of this dedication.
- Stay away from people and places who initiate evil dedication or renew it. This will include worldly activities such as certain festivals, concerts, et cetera. You will have to pray and let the Holy Spirit tell you the source of this evil and keep you from renewing it accidentally.
- Go for deliverance.
- Pray against satanic retaliation, and demonic regrouping.

Out of Nazareth

Can anything good come out of Nazareth?
Can anything good come out of your hometown?
Can anything good come out of your family?

The friends and groups, societies, and clubs you join make a difference. What are those organizations about? Not what is presented to the outside world as to what they are about, but what are the **secrets** of any *secret* society? Most likely, there are idols buried deep in those charters, else it wouldn't have to be a secret. Have you pledged or vowed to an idol, unawares—before accepting Christ, or even after? Then you have now joined up with another collective of people and since there are idols involved, there will be punishment, sooner or later. That could be collective, selective, partial or individual punishment.

Please say you do not want to be the one who is punished.

The church you become a member of --, you will share in the Grace of the local Body, and specifically you sit under the Grace of the head of that church, the pastor. Better look and pray that he is operating under Grace before you join that assembly.

What good comes out of that church? Do those who join *change*? Is there *lift*? Do they become more like Christ or not? Do they stay long? How's their health? Do they live long in that church? How are their family units? Are they married? How are their children? Are they being raised well, or are they brats? Don't just look at the pastor and his or her spouse but do look at them; you are sitting under their Grace--, their lack of Grace, and even their *dis*grace if that is their future. Are the people in your church comfortable, financially? Are they all broke? Are they all wealthy? What's going on in there?

If what happens to the people of that congregation is negative and not of God, then they are in captivity. Yes, even a church can be in collective captivity. Discern every *spirit*.

There are different kinds of captivity. There is selective, partial, individual, or collective captivity. Likewise, there are different kinds of deliverance from any of those types of captivities. One person can seek deliverance on their own, even if they are in a family, or the entire family can be delivered all at once. The family that prays together can be delivered together, depending on their faith, and their individual and corporate anointing.

People love to recruit members to their groups, clubs, or societies. When you connect with others you either add *your* grace to what they are planning to do, or they siphon your grace from you, whether you agree to it or not.

What happens to a family that is in collective captivity depends on the family's spiritual foundation. Is this a saved family? For how long? What generation of saved are you in your family? What covenants are in place in your bloodline? What altars are working against your family or *for* your family? Are there curses over your family? What idols are in your father's house? What do you owe to any *spirits,* powers, idols, or entities because of hidden or blatant idolatry?

What strongmen or strongwomen are up against you? Is there any household witchcraft? If you are marrying into a family of witches or warlocks – that's really not funny and you shouldn't take it lightly. Better find it out before getting married or connected to an occultic bloodline. If you marry a witch or a warlock, your child will automatically be a witch as soon as it is conceived and born. Period.

It is a common curse to be placed on a person that he or she only marry a witch or a warlock. You've probably heard too many men say that their Ex is a witch. Did they not see that *witchiness* before they married that person? Or are they just prone to hyperbole? According to Apostle Rodney Chipoyera, if you marry a witch, your destiny is shot; it's over. Yet, some are cursed, that all the men in a family, or all the women, or the whole family, to only marry witches or warlocks. These could be blind witches, undercover witches or out there in the open witches.

This is what I call a gentle witch who may or may not be blind to their own witchiness.

- They have witchy décor; such as witchy art.
- They have witchy items all over the house.

- They have witchy, occultic, or satanic tattoos all over themselves.
- Halloween is their favorite "holiday," and they do up the décor and the costumes for the day.
- They love wearing black, especially pointy nails and black nail polish.
- They believe in magic. Check their horoscopes regularly, love WitchTok, will go to diviners, tarot card readings, and the like, and say it is for entertainment.
- They tend to be very jealous, revengeful and petty. Witches and unrepentant sinners flow full force in the works of the flesh even though they serve other *spirits* rather than the Holy Spirit.

These are not necessarily ugly people. Many times, they are very handsome or beautiful--, it's part of their allure.

Simon Wasn't Simple

Simple Simon met a pieman,
Going to the fair;
Says Simple Simon to the pieman,
Let me taste your ware.
Said the pieman unto Simon,
Show me first your penny;
Says Simple Simon to the pieman,
Indeed I have not any…
(Nursery Rhyme, 1764)

That nursery rhyme is not about the Simon who was a wizard in the Bible. Neither was that wizard named Simon, simple. Bewitching is not child's play. Simon was nobody's dummy; Simon was running things.

In the book of Acts the people in Samaria are bewitched by a sorcerer named Simon. That bewitchment put them into collective captivity.

Simon was a wizard who was so strong in the occult that lesser witches didn't dare mess with him.

> Then Philip went down to the city of Samaria, and preached Christ unto them. … But there was a certain man, called Simon, which beforetime in the same city used sorcery, and bewitched the people of Samaria, giving out that himself was some great one: and all the people, both high and low, gave him their attention and exclaimed, "This man is the divine power known as the Great Power."
> Acts 8:5-6-9

Samaria was in captivity by Simon—well, by the devil through Simon. It was a *collective captivity* because the entire group of them, in this case, the city, was under his control. Simon wasn't an army or the general controlling any type of military force, naturally. Instead, he was one individual who had the ability to bring an entire city into bondage, or captivity, spiritually.

The Bible mentions in Ezekiel how 25 men sat at the gate and schemed and planned how to make that city their *cauldron* and have advantage for themselves and make the people do what they wanted those people to do. (Ezekiel 11)

Simon was one dude.

O foolish Galatians who hath bewitched you? Paul also asked the Galatians what their problem was. It seemed these folks were saved but they had started to believe some doctrine that was legalistic and not of God. The Judaists were feeding them information that was not true, but they believed it, so Paul also called them bewitched by this group of religious folks. This group put them in collective captivity also. (Galatians 3).

The point is that captivity of any kind can come by one or many, or by territorial *spirits* if the captivity is over an entire region, or by combinations of spirits and powers if a person is under more than one type of bondage.. Simon had the authority of territorial power and that's a lot of power. And that is why I asked where you were born or where you live now. Collective captivity is possible over regions and territories and that affects all the people in that geographical area. For example, whole areas vote Red or Blue in elections--, that's not always choice as one would think, it can be collective captivity. *Familiar spirits* in the region cause people to think alike, talk alike, look alike, dress alike, and even vote alike.

Witchcraft power on any level is very powerful if it is uncontested. It is unopposed when people don't believe that it is real, or that it exists. It is uncontested when the people don't stand up against it. It is uncontested when the people don't know that they are supposed to or even **can** stand up against it. It is uncontested when the people don't know *how to* stand up against it.

It is especially uncontested when the people, because of their own sin or other issues, are not in their proper position and authority, and therefore, spiritually, **cannot** stand up against witchcraft and break themselves free from it.

Don't oversimplify witchcraft or how to get out from under it.

Break Curses:

- Repent.
- Plead the Blood of Jesus.
- Break the evil covenant keeping the curse in place.
- Revoke the spell.
- Bind and send demons back to the sender.

Simon Says

In the children's game, Simon Says, the players must obey all commands that begin with the words "Simon says." Because thee Samaritans were under bewitchment the people of Samaria did what Simon **said**, whether they realized it or not.

I cannot tell you what the incantations of a Simon are, or may be, but know that there are plenty. Those incantations are usually done in secret (that's why it's called, *occult* – because it is hidden), so unless you're trained in the dark arts you don't know what Simon said – but if his chanting is empowered by the kingdom of darkness, and you don't have any defense against it, you may end up doing what Simon says.

Of note, evil enchanters will enchant the same thing over and over for hours and hours until they feel like or know that they will have their way against whomever or whatever they are chanting about.

That is called meditating. Meditating is not just sitting cross-legged shaping your finger and thumb into an O shape and humming a vowel.

Meditating is *murmuring*, speaking, and saying the same thing over and over again. Christians, that is what we are supposed to be doing by keeping our mind on Jesus, saying what He would say, and praying without ceasing. Whether or not we are defending ourselves against a witch or witchcraft, we should be doing that. Further, why do Christians wait until something happens in the natural before we even pray? Come on, saints! We need to get off the defensive and be on the offensive. The Word says we should be advancing the Kingdom of God, not just defending it.

Recently someone asked me, regarding a certain prayer that I prayed, why did I pray the same line over and over? Above is the answer. The Word of God says to do it. Plus, by importunity we can get our petitions granted from

God. This is private prayer, to God, not public spectacles to impress anyone.

So, when Simon or someone like a Simon is enchanting, we don't know exactly what Simon says, but we know he is saying either a lot, or the same thing over and over to an entity that is **not** God. When a witch, wizard, or warlock is enchanting they will say the same things over and over –to an idol, to any entity that is not God, and that is the definition of enchanting.

Some people say that there are no coincidences. Since there is nothing new under the sun, all "new" things must be inspired by someone or something. Christians would like to think that all things are inspired by God, but the devil can inspire things – too many things that men act out in this Earth. Simon says – Simon enchants, Simon curses, and Simon bewitches – by _saying_. And the people obey what Simon says.

They will turn their ears away from the truth and turn aside to myths. (2 Timothy 4:14)

There is something about humans that makes most want to believe a myth, a fairytale, or a lie rather than the truth. It could be from the early days of our upbringing where we have been raised on fairytales.

Walt Disney believed in magic. Sources say that all of Disney being about elves and fairies and magic is demonic. Disney has bewitched the whole world, and it starts with babies and toddlers. Parents, especially those who have been brought up in it believe this is fun and a rite of passage for little children. The Bible says we are to teach our children at all times, not let Disney, the TV, or the internet teach your children at all times.

There are people who take things away from you and then convince you that they are the person to help you find what they, themselves are hiding from you. Simon had convinced the Samaritans that he could help them with their problems – the problems that **he** created, and that is just like the devil.

Philip arrived in a city that was under collective captivity by Simon who had bewitched a whole city with demonic powers. Disney has bewitched far more than one city. Samaritans were so duped that they were calling on the powers of darkness to solve the problems that darkness had created in their lives. Instead of calling on God, they were seeking demonic powers or demonic solutions for life's problems.

Collective Captivity

Collective captivity is when all the members of a family, a group, a community, or a region are spiritual captives. This is evidenced by repeated **problems** in the family line, for example. It looks a lot like generational curses such as *like mother like daughter*, and *like father, like son.*

When illnesses run in a family, that is collective captivity. If your father had High Blood Pressure, for example, and for no real reason one or more of his children develop it – that is collective captivity. Especially when this dread disease happens at the same age for each of those afflicted.

A young man of a certain age died. Years later, his son also died at that exact same age.

Both died from the same heart-related condition. That was because of collective captivity. The last man left a son--, will the third son also die at that same age? Time will tell unless God intervenes.

God will intervene when you pray and ask Him to. Else is wishing and hoping. Else, is fantasy believing that you can *will* some spiritual oppression that is running in, and running your family to pass you by because you want it to.

My mother's mother died when my mother was five years old. It was never discussed, not even whispered of what she died of. None of my mother's children were five years old when my mother passed, having lived a long and productive life. The untimely death curse of the collective captivity in my mother's house was broken. Thank You, Jesus!

However, after my mother's mother died, my mother's father remained unmarried until after my mother turned 18 years old. When I see a pattern like this running in a bloodline, I consider not being married, happily married, or married for a long time to the wife of your youth a captivity issue. Especially when I look at my family's issues with marriage, anti-marriage, and divorce. Since my mother's father was quite a bit older than my mother's mother, that is another pattern of her father's house that could have been passed down to her children, me included. This could indicate a collective captivity or the proclivity for such.

Just because your family had certain things happen to them doesn't mean *you* have to follow the evil family pattern. You can't just wish your life would be better, you must do something about it --, in Christ.

Lateness in marriage is a curse, even though so many think it is their choice. Broken homes, poverty, lack of progress in life and failure are all curses, but Christ has made provision for your freedom!

Examples of Collective Captivity

Eli was from the priestly family of Aaron. God ordained him and his generation to be priests before Him, all the days of their lives. Eli's male offspring were sleeping with temple prostitutes. This displeased God greatly, so the fate that God pronounced fell upon the entire family. That was a family captivity created by the sins of those two boys.

God issued two types of curses on Eli's family line. There shall not be found an old person in his family, that means they will be dying young. The second part of the curse is that they will be poor and beg for bread, (1 Samuel 2).

Collective captivity is a curse placed upon a generational line because of the sin of one or more people.

Gehazi was cursed with leprosy from running after Naman and getting money from him after Elisha had refused the money. Elisha cursed him and said the leprosy of Naman shall cling unto thee and thy generation forever.

High blood pressure seems to run in people of color; that is collective captivity. It doesn't mean all of the Black race, but it can mean many. As a matter of fact, blood pressure numbers are different for Black men, than for other races. What is considered normal for Black men is high for others.

Never make a vow that you won't fulfill. Never get into evil covenants. That is why those people who do blood covenant and fail to fulfill their promise are in danger of collective captivity.

Research has shown that if a man goes to jail, his children too will also go to jail in time. Going to jail is a definite natural sign that a man is captive in the spirit.

A child was adopted at birth because his birth mother was very young, her *parents* were religious and didn't want to jeopardize their position *(image)* in their church, and the birth father was in jail. Before this adopted kid was 20 years old, living many states away, and not in touch with his birth father at all, he was also in jail. He's been locked up for about 10 years, now.

If your father is a polygamist, you are subject to the effects of polygamy and also to do the same. Polygamy is not just being married to more than one spouse, or more than one spouse at a time. Serial daters are polygamists. Serial cheaters are polygamists. Having one or more baby momma's or baby daddy's is also polygamy.

If your folks are hot in the pants, so will their children be. There may be promiscuity and eventually accidental pregnancy in your family. If papa was a rolling stone, then there will be rolling stones in that family. The boys will behave just like dad, and the girls may also.

Or, the girls will bring home a man just like dad. I told that to a rolling stone that I knew, and he smiled thinking that his daughter would bring home someone highly educated such as himself. Nope, that is not the promise – the idols over this behavior, the ones that enforce collective captivity will be sure that the man the daughter brings home will be a polygamist, rolling stone, just like her father, unless there is repentance and Christ is completely brought into this family.

Witchy parents, actually even one witchy parent will give birth to a witch: it's automatic, and, it's collective captivity. Of all the captives, a witch, warlock or a wizard are the most captive and they probably don't realize that they are.

You are the express image of your father. Is your father a drunkard, you too will become a drinker. Like father, like son. Is your father impoverished, you too will be poor unless you can break that heavy yoke by the Anointing of God and the Blood of Jesus.

The sins of the parents and ancestors, if not repented of, will locate the children. The family's blood will find the children no matter if they've been adopted, moved away, or even if the parents have gone on to Glory.

Children are often caught flat footed when they have to pay for things they didn't even buy and didn't know that a purchase had been made. Can we not see that blood is precious and should be protected, and not polluted? Sin pollutes the blood of a family. You are not just passing on your pretty eyes and thick hair and all-around good looks and smarts into your generations. You are passing on your BLOOD, and everything that is in it—not just the DNA and the genes, but also the *spiritual* stuff that is in your blood.

The wicked man may have repented and accepted Christ before he died and God will accept his repentance, and that man may be in Heaven right now. But the consequences, the iniquity stands, waiting for the children. Unless those children are fully in Christ and the iniquity has been forgiven.

Whatever you are going through today may be because of your own doing, or it is the result of your parental or ancestral sins. In addition to repenting for the sins of your folks, ask God to remove all iniquity. The devil keeps careful records of our sins to use against us later. Ask God to delete any files that stand against you in the spiritual world.

- I renounce every family, group, tribe, and collective captivity that I was born into by natural birth.

Break any curse of collective captivity upon your own generation. Work out your own salvation first, and then assist your family and friends. You must be born again and be a Protestant Christian to do this.

So many think when they get uncomfortable in their life that they can pop into a church or church service, get what is prepared for the saints of God and then pop back out into the world and continue doing what they were doing before. Nope, it doesn't work like that.

I heard a minister recently say that usually only about ½ the people in a church are even saved. Now, that's something to think about.

Deliverance is needed to break the chains that bind evil to your family. Confess the sins of your ancestors, parents, and yourself before God. Now you can break those bonds by the Fire of the Holy Ghost. Look into your family history--, if you see evil patterns, break the evil covenants and the curses that cause repetitive problems.

Do you see common diseases or infirmities in your family? Collective captivity must be broken.

Do you see wayward children? Then one or both parents must have done terrible things in the past, such as adultery, drunkenness, were part of a secret society or cult, or visited a witch, warlock, wizard, or diviner.

It's Not Hurting Anyone

The often-heard phrase, *It's not hurting anyone* that people use to justify the sin that a person wants to do can never be true. Unless what you are doing is **in** God, *of* God and sanctioned by God. Else, it could hurt everything.

All the ideas of man to get rich quick, famous, or get anything that God says not to touch, lead to evil. They lead to initiations and unrepented of, they lead to captivity. You need to get your ideas, directives, instructions and guidance from God, and God alone.

There will come a time to pay the piper. What do you think a person who owes the Piper will pay the Piper *with*?

Family members. Group members. Society members. Strangers if he can get a hold of them, but most often it is close folks. So, if family members are used, then this captivity gets in the bloodline. Family members, close associates, and illicit spouses (ex's) will submit your name for sacrifice to feed the idols (demons) of a collective captivity. It's why all the same awful stuff keeps happening in a group, or family. It is why things happen to one after the other in a collective.

Have you noticed the pattern of it happens to everyone except one? (Just asking.)

Idols want sacrifices.

The devil wants sacrifices.

If sacrifices are not given, then sacrifices can be taken. If they are not paid at all, *captivity* happens. Folks are put in a spiritual debtor's prison.

People who are so driven that they are willing to do anything, give anything are the most dangerous people in the world. There is nothing the devil offers that does not bring captivity; absolutely nothing.

We live in an anything goes society. The more outrageous a thing is the happier people are to try a thing. Folks don't care where the idea came from they just want to know if it works.

Repercussions are not of concern --, people just live for now, today, fame, and wealth. Yes, the devil makes enticing offers to people, he doesn't always come through, but he does entice, every day of the week.

Look at the bondages that your family members or relatives are in. See the pattern? That's collective captivity.

What about your special club, society, or group? Collective captivity.

What about your job? Yeah, you probably blame it all on the boss, but if it is not the boss, it's collective captivity.

What about your neighborhood? You have to look at the patterns. It is best to look at those patterns before you move to an area, but since you live there, take a good look. It may take discernment for you to see that what is happening to you is also happening to every person living in your neighborhood, or on your street.

That's just what happens here – it happens to everyone. If you can see that or say that, then that's collective captivity.

When Abimelech had Sarah in his palace, God was very displeased and shut up all the wombs in that place until Sarah was returned. Collective captivity is possible because of sin. It can be by God's decree, or by the devil getting permission from God as he did with Job. All of Job's first children died on the same day, in the same way. Collective captivity, folks.

People in cults are in collective captivity and the cult leader is the physical jailer over them. When they each drink the poison and die over time, that is collective captivity. If they all drink it on the same day and die together, that is still collective captivity.

If they don't drink poison but are invaded by people with guns and the compound gets shot up and burned and they all die, it is still because of collective captivity.

Of course, people who are not spiritual will not believe in evil patterns, they won't even look to see if anything unusual is happening. They will have some simple coincidental or other explanation to everything, to explain it away and keep it moving.

Got Cha!

Have you ever met anyone who loved *gotcha* moments? Legalists, authoritarians, stern disciplinarians come to mind. Satan comes to mind. He loves to capture God's children and he has many subtle, sudden, and evil ways to do it.

Here's one way that you may not have considered or suspected. Nightmares. Night terrors. Day terrors. Any trauma. The devil loves trauma. Two nights ago, I was minding my own business – sleeping. Terror came into a dream, I forced myself awake, but my heart was pounding…so I was *involved* in that dream, not just a jaded onlooker.

If sudden terror or sudden destruction or fear happens to you, it's for a reason. One such reason is for the devil to insert or leave behind some evil *spirit* to pollute or defile your soul. Here's what to pray:

- Lord, anything deposited in me, left in me when a certain evil *spirit* passed through or affected me when_____, or on _____ (name the day or event) happened, come out of my soul, and die, in the Name of Jesus. Amen.

Sadly, we live in an immoral society and people wear anything or next to nothing, or nothing out in public. This is very enticing to any gender. Sexual sin is a ***gotcha***, every day of the week, every hour of the day. Television and movies desensitize us to sexual immorality, in our *anything goes* world. Some seek out and look forward to tv or movie sex pretending innocence, saying things like, *"I didn't know that was in there."* They want illegal thrills for free.

But, saints of God, unexpected or shocking sex scenes are sudden attacks that can leave behind a demon of *lust* for example. They are initiations, they create soul ties and spiritual marriages. They create evil covenants that can lead to collective captivity.

Collective Money

I've seen this far too many times, and if you don't see anything wrong about this then you might be doing it. There is a fine line to balance this out. I've noticed where large families that may or may not describe themselves as close, or close knit will all seem to be emotionally, and/or financially *married* to each other to the exclusion of meeting new people and inviting or accepting them into the family. Many of those in the *close-knit described* family are not able to get married or maintain a marriage, successfully.

There was a man when his mother was on her deathbed told him to financially take care of his grown, married sister. He agreed since that was his mother and he was emotionally involved, possibly not knowing any better.

Since then – in the past 10 years both of them have divorced their respective spouses. The sister has never worked a job and the brother foots her bills. On her deathbed the mother *married* those two to each other. Did she do it purposefully, or ignorantly? The brother doesn't have sense enough to see it and get out of it even though it has dragged his marital and financial life. Further, having his sister all in his life in that way has affected his relationship with each of his children, negatively.

The sister is benefiting, so why should she try? This is pseudo polygamy, and it has created all of the problems of polygamy.

Most often this "sibling marriage" although it sounds totally incestuous is not sexually so, but it is the intermingling of souls and finances.

Sometimes the parents marry their own children themselves, by marrying their children's finances and earning potential. The parents may be the guiltiest of all, expecting the children, and especially the oldest child who as a teenager or very young adult to supply money to the household just because he got his first part-time job. This will drain the child of their finances and stop the child from being able to save or build for a future. It may even preclude the young adult from an education or marriage, which will lock him into the same life the parents had. Seriously, how can **one** person, who is maybe a high school graduate, make enough money to take care of a mother, father, himself, and other children in his family of birth? And then also build for his own future?

It's when your money doesn't have a designated purpose, a purpose will be decided for you. Especially when your money has not been assigned a Godly purpose, a worldly or demonic purpose will be given to it. Don't be a victim. Dedicate your money to God and give it Kingdom purpose.

The oldest child is not a parent, should not be parentized, and should not be taking care of the siblings – if the parents are alive and well. The older siblings should not be taking care of the minor siblings, or the parents for that matter. Yes, free will offerings --- bless your folks on special occasions because you want to, but no one should have to pay for the clothing, medical treatment, et cetera of a sibling because the parents are or feel strapped. What money were they using before that oldest child even got a job?

This keeps that child tied to the financial altar of poverty of the parents. It keeps him or her from being able to leave home because they can't afford to. AND, if he or she ever marries, they cannot cleave to their spouse because the birth family is still pulling on them. If ever they ask their older brother or sister for money and that sibling says, *I'm married now, I've got to ask my husband, (or wife)"* all hell may break loose.

Their money, their finances are captive, captured by the parents and siblings of their birth. This is financial collective captivity. Finances are part of the gift that the husband gives his own wife and children. The family altar is kept burning with loving, free will offerings from each marital partner. If the family of origin has the money of either marital partner, that is the same as saying, you can go into your marriage, and you can even live in another house – but leave the money here with us. That is the same as Pharoah saying that the Hebrew slaves could go up to worship, but they could not take their livestock. It's like saying, *You can go to the mall, but you cannot take a credit card, a checkbook, or cash.*

Power Against Collective Captivity

When the young adult who may have just started working tries to get out of the financial captivity that their family of origin has roped them into, in order to establish themselves and establish covenant with God and build their own family and life – something, or someone--, some need will pull them back in, or try to pull them back.

God established covenant with Abraham and made covenant with Abraham, not with Lot, and not with all the other members of Abraham's family. God established covenant with Moses. Aaron wasn't with him. God establishes covenant with individuals alone. Abraham tithed in Levi by giving a tenth of all to Melchizedek. Abraham didn't give a tenth of all to his parents, siblings, or even to Lot who tagged along probably to see what he could get. When a young person gets married they make covenant with their spouse, all previous soul ties must be broken.

We know from Scripture that Abraham took care of about 300 families – that's how rich he was. But what Abraham did was part of his divine purpose. If he were *broke*, he wouldn't have been able to do that and fulfill destiny.

More than once, God sent a prophet with a prophet's reward to widow women and poor folks. God did not bind the chosen one to destitution with their relatives. He called them out from their birthplace and birth families. If God could do that for Abraham, he could also do it for each of Abraham's kin. But look at Lot, when Sodom and Gomorrah were destroyed, do you think Lot got out with his wealth and cattle? Nope, he got out with just his life. God established covenant with Abraham, and Abraham, with God. Lot didn't. My point is, no matter what you give people who **you** choose or folks who demand money from you, but God didn't choose that set up, unless they have a proper covenant with God, will they lose it, anyway? (That's another whole book.)

When folks who are called of God try to establish covenant with God, someone in their

58

family may try to tag along to get in on it, or the devil will sponsor someone calling that person back into the "family" dynamics.

Every time.

I've seen this in many impoverished cultures.

It's also why some parents, especially mothers, won't let their sons go. They expect their son to now be their breadwinner, their retirement plan, even though their husband may still be there. These mothers want what the young man's **wife** should be getting. She may guilt trip and manipulate her child to the max to get her way, and that is witchcraft. A married child's money if not for the mother, or father to get from their child, and it keeps this man unmarried, or unsuccessfully married.

The Word says to leave and cleave. Your finances should be comingled with your spouse, not entangled with your family of birth after you get married.

An independent husband desired to take care of his wife and two children, and he was pretty successful at that. But, his wife was used to more and whenever her husband wouldn't get her what she wanted, she'd ask her birth parents and they'd just send her whatever she asked for. This emasculated and angered the dutiful husband. That married daughter who had teenaged children was still tied to her birth family's financial altar. Granted, her dad was well off, so she wanted to enjoy the financial grace that she was used to. The man she married was in a different financial category—that of his family of birth and it was one of less than she was used to. Yes, that is a form of captivity that she did not want to participate, or suffer in.

Household Issues

There is no attack that happens in your life from strangers, that someone in your family has not consented to. Household witchcraft? They may not realize they are giving consent for other witchcraft to come into the family, but they are. They make themselves the contact point for other witchcraft, knowingly, or unknowingly.

Household witchcraft is from people who are usually related to you, but people who live in the same house you live in. Brothers, sisters, mother, father, grands, and et cetera comprise the average *household*.

She was 16 or 17 – she got connected with a witch. That was the year that family started going through hell. And it hasn't stopped up until now. She built some type of altar which she lied and said was a Buddhist altar, as bad as that is, since all in that house were raised Christian, the family now suspects it was an occultic or witchcraft altar.

Looking back, they can now see when the unraveling of the family began. The sin of that one child put the family into collective captivity which may have been over and above whatever captivity the family was already oppressed by.

- Every attack of my enemies where I've been handed over by relatives and relations--, I declare today, you will not hand me over, you will not arrest me to hand me over, ever again, in the Name of Jesus.
- Every family meeting which is a plot to arrest me or hand me over, I will not attend that meeting--, whether it is a holiday, a wedding, a birthday, or a funeral. I will not attend that meeting, in the Name of Jesus.

Not only does it take a village – a village can take it all, if you are not prayerful.

More Relatives?

You also become *related* to people by sex. Goes into equals married. When you have sex with a person, they are now related to you, by blood. Now the two of you share an evil covenant that, of course, the devil is in, but by that sexual act, you've given that person and the devil access to you.

Even after you break up with that person, whether you married them or not, that now gives your "ex" access to you, access to your very soul. The only way out is to repent, renounce the sin and be sure to break every evil covenant formed between the two of you, and also break the soul tie(s).

You are connected to every undenounced sexual partner and they are connected to you – by **blood**. These relationships and entanglements open doors to the enemy. Sex outside of marriage is grievous to God, but also leaving that type of relationship in anger, bitterness, or with soul ties of any kind opens so many doors to the devil that you should be able to feel the drafts.

The demonic and occultic need someone in your family as a door opener. If you don't open the doors to the enemy, they will try other ways in--, such as the teenager with the evil altar that she blatantly brought into her parents' Christian home. The sad thing about that is the family disregarded her actions as frivolous and not serious.

No weapon formed against you shall prosper. Saints of God, stop helping the devil *form* weapons against you.

My Father, disgrace the human beings that are working with Satan to trouble my life, in the Name of Jesus.

My Father, disgrace the human beings that are working with Satan to destroy Your purposes in my life, in the Name of Jesus.

I release myself from every evil family pattern of poverty--, from every collective captivity of my birth family, or any group, society, club, fraternity, sorority, or organization that I am in, in the Name of Jesus.

Every prosperity paralysis from household wickedness, come out with all your roots by Fire, in Jesus' Name.

Oppression agenda of my family idol, die, in the Name of Jesus.

Every sacrifice my family idol has received from my enemies, let that sacrifice fail to work, in the Name of Jesus.

I break all evil patterns in my life, my family's life, in the Name of Jesus.

Evil patterns, I rebuke you in the Name of Jesus.

Break Soul Ties:

By the cross of Jesus Christ, I break every soul tie and every unholy bond with ___. I command their human spirit bound back to their body, and I send all of their sin and warfare and corruption bound back to the throne of Christ in their life. I forbid them or their warfare or their sin to transfer to me. And I allow only the love of God, only the bond of the Holy Spirit, between us.

In the name of the Lord Jesus Christ. Amen
Adapted from www.wildatheart.org

Collective Bondage

Prayers to break collective bondage whether generational, ancestral, or familial must be employed to break bondage, and captivity over your own life and also prophetically break out of collective captivity so things do not transfer to your children and your *children's* children. You need to get out of evil patterns and evil yokes as soon as you become aware of them.

So, what if your siblings don't like you anymore once you're delivered? If you stay in captivity, you will be bound for death and destruction. At least if one of you breaks free there is hope, *more hope* for the bloodline. Perhaps now that you're free you can break others out of spiritual jail.

I personally love to be in a deliverance service whether I am called up or not. When the anointing flows for deliverance, the same anointing that can deliver the person at the altar can deliver any and all of us who are present in the service. That anointing can even deliver those who have friends or family members present in the service who are standing in for them.

We never disparage deliverance for another person. As a matter of course, we pray for their deliverance. If the prophet, apostle, or deliverance minister calls out something that you don't have, stand in the Presence anyway because God may be delivering you prophetically, so we won't even need to stand in that prayer line. We can be delivered on the pew, at our house--, anywhere and at any time that God says. God could deliver us from what we don't even know we have.

Break Bondages:

- Plead the Blood of Jesus.
- Bind the demonic *spirit* and powers behind the bondage.
- Break the evil covenant keeping the bondage in place.
- Revoke the spell behind the bondage.
- Dismantle, deprogram, and scatter the bondage.

Warfare Prayers

Lord, forgive all the sins of my parents and ancestors, in the Name of Jesus.

Blood of Jesus, break every family, ancestral and generational curse in my family.

Lord, I renounce all evil and idolatrous oaths I have made. Lord we repent of idolatry and sins against You. Break curses over my brothers and sisters who are in this group, society, fraternity, or sorority with me, in the Name of Jesus.

Lord, break the curses over my house, street, block, neighborhood, community, city, state, country, or all over the world, in the Name of Jesus.

Lord, break the curses over my culture, race, and gender, in the Name of Jesus.

Blood of Jesus blot out the iniquity of parental and ancestral sins, in the Name of Jesus.

Every power of evil directed against me, return to sender, in the Name of Jesus.

Lord, release me from all and any kind of collective captivity, in the Name of Jesus.

Lord, let every word curse spoken against me backfire, in the Name of Jesus.

Lord, release me from all inherited bondage, in the Name of Jesus.

Lord, let Your Axe of Fire take down the evil foundation of my life and destroy every evil plantation within it, in the Name of Jesus.

Anything evil transferred to me in the womb, I don't want it, I destroy it, in the Name of Jesus. Blood of Jesus, flush it out, in Jesus' Name.

Blood of Jesus and Holy Ghost Fire, cleanse and restore every organ in my body, and reverse all damage, in the Name of Jesus.

I break every evil collective captivity covenant, in the Name of Jesus.

I vomit out all evil spiritual food, every evil consumption that I have ever been fed in my entire life, in the Name of Jesus.

All foundational strongmen attached to my life be bound and paralyzed, in the Name of Jesus.

Every root of collective captivity, I destroy, I uproot you by the Fire Axe of God, in the Name of Jesus.

- Ancestral curses
- Parental curses
- Generational curses
- Familial curses
- Envious sibling, polygamous, or associates' witchcraft and rivalry
- Demonic incisions and marks
- Dream pollution
- Dream initiations
- Demonic blood transfusion
- Fellowship with family idols.
- Fellowship with evil human agents
- Ungodly manner of conception.
- Evil dedication
- Demonic marriage
- Demonic sacrifice.
- Inherited health problems, infirmity
- Evil laying on of hands.
- False pastors
- False prophets

- Wrong exposure to sex
- Exposure to witches, warlocks, wizards, diviners.
- Polygamy.
- Stuck families.

Captives Are Stuck

I've seen both individuals and entire families stuck in grief. Transitioning to the next realm, or at least out of the Earth realm should be handled, I believe, biblically.

Marriage is of God. In the Bible, when somebody died, GOD gave them a new spouse. Didn't Ruth get with Boaz? Wasn't God putting Onan with Tamar after Er was dead? Wasn't Shelah expected to become Tamar's husband after Onan was killed? Get-a-new-spouse was built into that culture.

The grief process is hard, but the Bible shows where God gave the people 30 days to mourn for Moses and then keep it moving.

Terah, (Abraham's father) grieved for his another of his sons who had died, and stayed stuck in that place. Because the family was moving together, but Terah became stuck. God had to call Abraham OUT of Ur, else Abraham would have stayed there over grieving for his lost brother too.

The Bible says that the dead know nothing, and we have to be careful that we don't go into ancestral worship, over-grieve, or pine for the dead. This is a slippery slope because Grief has a strong pull -- it wants to pull the griever and over-griever also into death. While it is tough, I believe, while not disrespecting God or the dead, we have to keep on living. Else, humans get stuck.

After the death of a family member or loved one, families think that love is what is keeping them sad. When does Love make a person sad? 1 Corinthians 13 tells us what love is. Yes, I'll rehearse it here: because nowhere in it is love SAD, or sadness, grieving, over-grieving, or being stuck. Nowhere.

Love is patient and kind. Love is not jealous or boastful or proud [5] or rude. It does not demand its own way. It is not irritable, and it keeps no record of being wronged. [6] It does not rejoice about injustice but rejoices whenever the truth wins out. [7] Love never gives up, never loses faith, is always hopeful, and endures through every circumstance.

Yes, Love lasts forever, real agape love. Don't let soul ties last forever. don't let inappropriate grief last forever.

> Three things will last forever—faith, hope, and love—and the greatest of these is love.
> (1 Corinthians 13:9)

More on this topic in my book, **Seasons of Grief**.

Lord, Disgrace Them

But upon mount Zion shall be deliverance, and there shall be holiness; and the house of Jacob shall possess their possessions, (Obad. 1:17)

Prayer points in this book are designed for deliverance from evil family patterns, evil bondage, yokes, curses, and covenants. You need that because even if you live in a developed country right now, you don't know what your ancestors did. They could have sold your destiny and not even realized that they did it. They could have innocently done what everyone else in the community was doing. They could have done something that was presented to them as innocent, with no repercussions--, but that may have been a lie they fell for because they were greedy, or desperate, or hungry. Everything everyone does affects everyone--, somehow and at some time – good or bad.

Christ hath redeemed us from the curse of the law, being made a curse for us: for it is written, Cursed is every one that hangeth on a tree: That the blessing of Abraham might come on the Gentiles through Jesus Christ; that we might receive the promise of the Spirit through faith.
Gal. 3:13-14

Lord, I pray for Mercy, in the Name of Jesus.

My Father and my God, have Mercy on me and my family, in the Name of Jesus.

Collective captivity of my father's house affecting my life, break by Fire, in the Name of Jesus.

Curses working against my family line break by Fire, in the Name of Jesus.

Any curse working against my family line, break by Fire, in the Name of Jesus.

Suffer Them Not to Speak!!!

If you are in captivity, then there are evil altars crying out against you. These altars could be from your father's house... many times what is fighting us is **in** our homes.

Whatever is happening at the evil altars on your father's house is affecting you negatively. Whoever is priesting at those altars, and they keep sacrificing on those altars --- if your name is mentioned, or has ever been mentioned at that altar, then that altar is still looking for you.

- You must pray for **DISCONNECTION** from the altars of your father's house.

When Jesus was casting out demons, He told His Disciples to suffer not the demons to speak. That is practical deliverance protocol. But demons speak from evil altars. If we silence the altar, we silence the demons, and not just one or two at a time, but every demon assigned to enforce evil covenants and curses from that particular evil altar.

We think *not suffer them to speak* means don't let demons speak—and it does. But demons are sent out because of evil covenants that create curses. Evil altars are the reasons for that. As long as evil altars are speaking, they will be sending out decrees and commands to sponsor evil into the lives of individuals, groups, societies, families and even churches.

Suffer not the evil altars to speak. Silencing evil altars is accomplished by power that is greater than the altar. A greater sacrifice, a greater dedication, greater faith, and by the Blood of Jesus, the Fire of the Holy Spirit.

Pray for exemption for whatever else they would speak in the future, including calling your name.

Connection to a parent comes via the blood. Connection to any random person that **you've made into your (illegal) spouse** comes through idolatrous, ritual sex. And, that sex is any illicit, illegal sex, with any *whosoever*.

Any power that curses any Godly collective that you are in, that curse must be broken, in the Name of Jesus. If you are in an ungodly or illegal collective, you must renounce membership with it, repent and get out of that group. You can't bless a group, sect, society, or cult that God has cursed as idolatrous.

Collective Delays

Collective delays, family delays come with collective captivity.

Collective delays can come as a result of whom you've chosen to pal around with --, if your favorite people are the slackers in your school who never do their homework, or get it turned in on time – you will suffer with that collective.

Those with whom you have chosen to team up with at work … you've formed an affiliation, an alliance with them. Forced or other, a collective is formed.

A new employee enters a job, but she brings the *spirit of delay* with her. While working for this company, she yokes up with every new employee that comes to work there. Soon the newest employee will follow the lead of this **bad** employee who is not getting pay increases, bonuses or perks because of their bad work performance. Really the original, bad employee is hanging on to her job by the skin of her teeth. This clique-forming employee is forming a collective that will delay the increases and promotion of every new employee that joins that company, creating *collective delays*.

Of note, the new employees are all told, do **not** follow that person – do not do what they do or as they do. But without their own level of confidence or independence the weak ones follow the bad employee and end up stagnant or fired.

That company wanted to terminate the bad employee, but now they use her as a way to evaluate new hires, but to the negative.

There are yokes of delays and bondages of delays.

This bad employee fosters delay, yet all the employees that came after her believe she is a leader because she was there first and asserts herself as a leader although she has no leadership skills, except for her junior level, possibly blind witchcraft. She can't even lead herself, for goodness sakes, but she has like Simon the sorcerer, she has convinced new employee after new employee to follow her, and the weaker souls do. When you're the candidate looking to work at a company or the new hire at that business, look to see what comes out of that business. How are the employees there? Do they prosper? Is there lift? Do their lives change favorably? Is it the individual employee who fails, or is the company holding them down? These are good questions to ask and learn the answer to.

Discern every *spirit*. Is one *"Simon"* holding the company captive? Who is it? If it is not the head of that company, then it would be safe to work there, just don't follow the person causing or fostering delay in promotion at that job.

She's delayed in everything she does. She is late for work most days. She doesn't finish projects on time. Worse, she makes excuses using thinly-veiled lies that she thinks are ironclad when every one of the bosses can see through the fabrications. This employee has accepted their delayed lifestyle. Many humans do and they now call it laid back, when really it is delayed. Humans excuse inactivity against chronic delay as being laid back.

Folks, complacency and being laid back will get you defeated in life.

The family where everything is delayed, suspect that ancient altars are projecting against that family.

Whenever there is a delay, it is because of an objection being levied against your success or promotion from your father's house. Delay because some jealous or hateful person is objecting.

Inherited delay of my father's house, , I am in Christ. Break off my life, in the Name of Jesus.

Every evil power that I have confronted that has not been removed because of delay, be removed now, by the power in the Blood of Jesus

Every demonic and satanic delay on a technicality--, be removed by the power in the Blood of Jesus, in the Name of Jesus.

Distant Relatives, Distant Altars

Any relatives that I know nothing about…distant relatives, relatives in distant lands, cultures who don't even know Christ, the Lord Jesus shut down your evil, idol worship, or wishes, incantations against me, in the Name of Jesus.

Any brothers and sisters, or other relatives that I know nothing about who may be the result of my father's or mother's polygamy, who are wishing ill against me because of jealousy or hatred, the Lord Jesus shut down your evil wishes against me, in the Name of Jesus.

Hometown witchcraft, folks from the village or the town who knew me when, who secretly never wanted me to leave or be successful, the Lord Jesus shut you down in your evil desires against me, in the Name of Jesus.

Time-sensitive curses, or programmed curses (through Triangular Powers) --, the sun the moon, the stars, the Earth--, any programming against or delaying my success, promotions or destiny – I deprogram it, in the Name of Jesus.

Earth O Earth, evil delays programmed, written into the Earth against my life, wherever I have gone I have received delays, any evil programmed into the Earth, I deprogram it, in the Name of Jesus.

I deprogram every evil incantation from the sun, moon, stars, Earth, water, even into the wind, all the elements, I deprogram it, in the Name of Jesus.

Break Free

Make haste, O God, to deliver me; make haste to
help me, O LORD. Psalm 70:1

When you are no longer okay to just go with the flow and do what everyone else in your group or family is doing, then you will ask the Lord for deliverance. And why not speedy deliverance?

God cares about what you are going through. Jesus was touched with the feelings of our infirmities. He knows how hard it is to go *through*, and how hard it is for you to go through what you are going through.

Coming into the presence of God though, one must observe the Law of Approach. You can't just step to God any kind of way you want.

God not only intends that you be free from captivity and bondage and yokes, but He promises to fight your battles for you. Don't get this wrong, saints of God, it doesn't mean that you have nothing to do once you accept Salvation. Remember Salvation gives a person the opportunity to *become* a Son of God.

Do you think God would have captive sons?

Do you think God would have sons who are not prospered in their souls?

If God says that He gives us prosperity to establish covenant with us. That tells me that God establishes covenant with us and we become sons. God would not have a child that He cannot be in covenant with. Being in covenant is a good thing because it means the stronger of the covenant will help the weaker. We are the weaker and God is the strongest. But this does not mean that He will forever breast feed or spoon porridge into our mouths. We must grow up and be able to get ourselves out of problems, especially the problems we have created by our own sin and choices.

Additionally, we have power, revelation, authority, and ability to get ourselves out of captivity, or at least know how to approach God to ask for His Divine assistance to get out of messes that our ancestors have gotten us into.

Why would God do this? Leave us to help ourselves get out of such binds?

Because that is what *sons* of God do.

Jesus was the Perfect Man; He was the Son in whom God was well pleased. Therefore, we must look to see what Jesus would do. We look in the Word of God, pray, and also listen to hear what the Holy Spirit says in order to get out of these spiritual problems.

Man is not inherently good; he is inherently evil, although most think they are "good people." The devil is the evilest and he is an influencer; he influences those who are inherently evil to be even more evil, and to do evil. He sets traps, he deceives, he snares, and we have to get out of those traps. If we are wise, we seek deliverance from God to be returned from captivity.

Of course, you know he only captures people to kill and destroy them. It not to entertain mankind, teach us to do tricks, or give us anything that is good; it is to kill.

Now you can see there must be an urgency to get out of captivity---, your *hide* is on the menu to be consumed.

No one is immune to what I've described, unless you are in Christ and that means **fully in** Are you *in* Him? Have you enthroned Him?

God is our Protector. He does not get tricked by the devil; humans do. If we walk in the way, the path that God says we won't get caught. But that is the problem, either man knows not the way of the Lord, or he can be disobedient and go his own way. The snares, the traps, the land mines, folks, are OFF God's path for your life.

This is why life can be so full of trouble. Man steps out of the plan of God for his life and all struggles and destruction await him. A person wants to do it his way, and that is usually by the flesh.

When a man's way doesn't work, he usually is enticed by, and drawn into other flesh ideas from other people. How did that rich guy do it? How about that one? How about that rich woman? So they try the ways of other **people**, still not trying the way of God. Our Father gives us power to get wealth so that He may establish covenant with us.

If you get wealth from the devil, who do you think you've established covenant with?

When a person steps into the flesh or into a devil deal, he is initiated into evil and most often not just by himself or for himself. Everything you get from the devil, and there' still no guarantee that you will actually get it, but everything you try to get from the devil costs you everything. Everything now, and into your future.

Witches, warlocks—the devil, *spirits* in general work outside of time. Flesh is the only thing subject to time. So a man's deal with the devil in the year 1605 can still be in effect right now, this year, unless someone has broken it. That initiation, that iniquity includes captivity and a bloodline or a people or people group—not just an individual. So that thing that you are doing that you think is not hurting anyone is initiating everyone – your entire bloodline.

Evil Spiritual Yoke

Being in an evil spiritual yoke is still captivity – it's just that you're on parole or in a half-way house. You're free to get a job, but the pharoahic spirit lording over that yoke is not to let you get but so far. You won't get far because among other things, that yoke is like a leash—if it is visible to you, or if it's invisible, it's like an ankle bracelet that's hidden under your pants leg.

You are *out of spiritual jail--*, but you're not, spiritually speaking.

The poor are under the yoke of the rich. If the rich are ruling politically speaking.

If the richest person in your family is not saved, and you are not all in Christ, you are under their yoke. The rich rule over the poor. If everyone in your family is poor except one person, that one person may be spiritually using the rest of you, whether he or she even knows it or not. All the females in a family dream of the same spirit husband – it means you are all under captivity and yoked – all under the same familial yoke.

If there is one person doing well in your family, but the rest are not--, look deeply to discover why. It doesn't mean to hate that person or devise evil against him or her. It could be that they are doing things according to the Word of God and God is blessing that person.

Ask God.

Act accordingly. <u>You</u> could be the problem; you could be your own problem.

Break Evil Yokes:

- Plead the Blood of Jesus.
- Bind the demonic *spirit* and powers behind the yokes.
- Break the evil covenant keeping the yoke in place.
- Revoke the spell behind the yoke.
- Dismantle, deprogram, and destroy the yoke.

Loose Me, Lord

Getting loosed from collective captivity requires that you pray with determination and force. The Kingdom of Heaven suffers violence, and the violent take it by force. Getting released from collective captivity means working on your spiritual, family, ancestral foundation, and it is not child's play.

When you are dealing with foundation, as with a house, you've got to take off all the décor, the pretty stuff, the siding, the roof even, and strip that house down to the studs. From that you dig up the subfloor and now you work on the foundation. Most of the time this takes a pickaxe or a jack hammer. Foundation is not just the location, foundation is usually made of the hardest, strongest material known to man to make sure that building stands.

Furthermore, the foundation goes deep. The taller the building the deeper the foundation. This is the reason we look back at our ancestors, do spiritual mapping and find out as much as we can about the roots of our foundation.

We want the edifice to remain if it is of God. We want it to last for generations, that's why the foundation is deep.

The devil is the same way, he wants his funky foundations and polluted foundations to remain as well.

This is going to take some sweat, saints of God. It will take Repentance. Cover yourself with the Blood of Jesus.
I loose myself from any inherited bondage in Jesus' Name.

O Lord, send Your Axe of Fire to the foundation of my life and destroy every evil plantation, in the Name of Jesus.

Let the blood of Jesus flush out from my system every inherited satanic deposit, in the Name of Jesus.

I release myself from the grip of any problem transferred into my life from the womb, in the Name of Jesus.

Let the Blood of Jesus and the Fire of the Holy Ghost cleanse every organ in my body, in the

Name of Jesus.

I break and loose myself from every collective evil covenant, in the Name of Jesus.

I break and loose myself from every collective curse, in the Name of Jesus.

I vomit every evil consumption that I have been fed with as a child, in the Name of Jesus.

I command all foundational strongmen attached to my life to be paralyzed, in the Name of Jesus.

Let any rod of the wicked rising up against my family line be rendered impotent for my sake, in the Name of Jesus.

I cancel the consequences of any evil local name attached to my person, in the Name of Jesus.

Ancestral sin, especially sins of money, illegal sex, addictions come out with all your roots, in the Name of Jesus.

Destroy Family Captivity

How many people in your family are living the very <u>same</u> life that your parents--, one or both of them, lived? Good or bad. If it's good, then there's no problem, you are walking in the blessings of your parents and ancestors. But if the same disappointments, failures, frustrations, and let downs are happening to the children that happened to the parents, that is collective captivity.

Some ministers say that the entire family needs to be together to break out of collective captivity, but sometimes that is not possible for any number of reasons. So, you are going to pray because you are now aware of the familial problems, and you are ready to break out of collective captivity.

After you break out, you still may go back and minister to the other captives, if they desire to break free, as well. This in no way disrespects parents or ancestors. You must be fully in Christ to get out, though. Were your folks all in Christ and just made a mistake or two? Or were your folks completely unsaved and that's why you all are in this iniquity?

Some signs of familial collective captivity:

1. Shortened life spans.
2. Health problems, especially the same health problem running through generations of people.
3. Polygamy.
4. Sexual deviations and perversions.
5. Cheating spouses.
6. Occultism and witchcraft in the family.
7. Lazy husbands where wives are the breadwinners.
8. No marriages. Unsuccessful marriages, Multiple marriages, delayed marriages, or divorces.
9. No children, reproductively barren.
10. Poverty, lack, insufficiency; financially barren.

Fire Prayers

Holy Ghost Fire, fall, in the Name of Jesus.

Holy Spirit, you are the Spirit of Deliverance, come into our midst today, in the Name of Jesus.

Lord, let my first fruits offerings and free will sacrifices cry me out of every evil dedication, in the Name of Jesus.

Lord, reveal Yourself to me, to our family, in the Name of Jesus. Come in Your Power and deliver us, O Lord.

Lord, manifest Yourself, manifest Your Glory in our lives, in Jesus' Name.

We go down to our foundation, today. Lord, let the battles of our family foundation die, in the Name of Jesus.

Ancestral and inherited battles in my life and my family's life, die by thunder fire in the Name of Jesus.

The God who answers by Fire, be God and answer by Fire today, in the Name of Jesus.

All inherited spiritual problems in my life, die in the Name of Jesus.

Every frustration, delay and destruction in my parents life that is trying to come into my life, die, in the Name of Jesus.

Ancestral battles in my life and family, die now by Fire, in the Name of Jesus.

Household witchcraft, stand down, in the Name of Jesus. (X5)

O God, arise and let all my enemies be scattered, in the Name of Jesus.

O God arise and contend with every enemy that is contending with me, in the Name of Jesus.

Every battle of collective captivity, die against me, now, in the Name of Jesus.

Every financial battle of collective captivity, die, in the Name of Jesus.

I separate myself from the collective, in the Name of Jesus, by the Blood of Jesus. I am in Christ. I am all in Christ.

Evil patterns of collective captivity in my family's foundation, cease against me, in the Name of Jesus.

Every curse of untimely death in my family, scatter by Fire, in the Name of Jesus.

Every curse of poverty in my family, die, in the Name of Jesus.

Every curse of infirmity in my family assigned at any time in my life, die, in the Name of Jesus.

Every pattern or assignment of death and tragedy in my family, scatter by Fire, in the Name of Jesus.

Evil powers of death operating in my family, die, in the Name of Jesus.

Every messenger of death, hell, or the grave, see the Blood of Jesus and pass over and then die, in the Name of Jesus.

Every evil pattern against my destiny, roast by Fire, in the Name of Jesus.

Evil giants, you don't scare me anymore, I am in Christ. The Lord Jesus rebuke you, scatter, and then drop dead, in the Name of Jesus.

I disconnect myself, my life from all satanic clocks, calendars, plans and patterns, in the Name of Jesus.

Any food initiation in my system by any witch, any satanist, or any captor that captured me and my family, no matter how or when it happened. come out, by Fire! Catch fire! Catch Fire, in the Name of Jesus.

Evil familial curses of any name or description, be broken by Fire, in the Name of Jesus.

Every devil or demon sent to enforce any familial curse against me, be bound and paralyzed in the Name of Jesus. Heavenly Hosts, take them away, declaring failed assignment, in the Name of Jesus.

Every pattern of failure, DIE, in the Name of Jesus.

Holy Ghost Fire, burn away every sexual, polluted, perverted, abnormal, and ungodly behavior, in the Name of Jesus. (X5)

Sexual immorality, sexual impurity, sexual disobedience, ritual sex desires, die, in the Name of Jesus.

Collective patterns of flesh works and sin in my family, die in me, die in every family member who desires to be set free, in the Name of Jesus.

Destructive anger in my family, die, in the Name of Jesus.

Every marker for flesh works and evil activities in my blood as a result of inheritance, die, in the Name of Jesus.

Jezebel or any *witchcraft spirit* in my soul, and in my family, die, in the Name of Jesus.

Every idol of my father's house polluting my spiritual walk with Christ, die, in the Name of Jesus.

Every inherited idol in my soul, die out by the Blood of Jesus.

Every ancestral *spirit* or power imparting its evil nature to me, be destroyed, in Jesus' Name.

Lord, give me the overcomer's anointing, in the Name of Jesus.

Lord, redeem the time, restore the years, repair all damage done in my life by collective captivity, in the Name of Jesus.

Lord, reverse all losses in my life due to collective captivity, in Jesus' Name.

Lord, return all divine connections, in Jesus' Name.

Lord, return all divine opportunities in my life lost due to being in collective captivity, in the Name of Jesus.

Every evil word spoken against me or my family, backfire, in the Name of Jesus.

Any confusion in my life, especially at the edge of breakthrough, I return you to sender, in the Name of Jesus.

Every evil arrow in my life, I return to sender, in the Name of Jesus.

Every pattern caused by idol worship, die in the Name of Jesus.

Every idol in my soul, die, in the Name of Jesus.

Every evil monitoring *spirit*, gadget, device, or other technology, be rendered useless against me, and unrepairable, in the Name of Jesus.

Every witch involved in the collective captivity of me or my family, the Lord says we should not suffer you to live, let your powers die, in the Name of Jesus.

Blood of Jesus, fight for me and my family, in the Name of Jesus.

Spirit of the enemy released on me by inherited covenants, be separated from me by the power in the Blood of Jesus.

Spirit of the enemy released on me by evil gates of my father's house, be separated from me by the power in the Blood of Jesus.

I seal these prayers and declarations across every timeline…

Every retaliation planned or attempted against me because of these prayers, backfire 7X in the Name of Jesus.

AMEN.

Dear Reader

Don't lose heart because of where you were born, what family you were born into or who your family or ancestors are.   God has provided a way of escape.

.

Amen.

Dr. Marlene Miles

Other books by this author

AK: The Adventures of the Agape Kid

AMONG SOME THIEVES

Ancestral Powers

Battlefield of Marriage (The)

Blindsided: *Has the Old Man Bewitched You?*
https://a.co/d/5O2fLLR

Churchzilla, The Wanna-Be, Supposed-to-be Bride of Christ https://a.co/d/1QcTblF

Demons Hate Questions

Devil Weapons: Unforgiveness, Bitterness,…

https://a.co/d/hGIhOXc

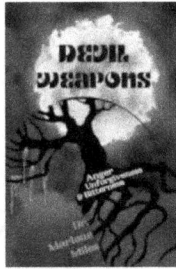

Dream Defilement

Don't Refuse Me, Lord (4 book series)

Every Evil Bird

Evil Touch

Fantasy Spirit Spouse

FAT Demons (The): *Breaking Demonic Curses*

The Fold (5 book series)

      The Fold (Book 1)

      Name Your Seed (Book 2)

      The Poor Attitudes of Money (3)

      Do Not Orphan Your Seed (4)

      For the Sake of the Gospel (5)

Gates of Thanksgiving

got HEALING? Verses for Life

got LOVE? Verses for Life

got HOPE? Verses for Life

got money?

How to Dental Assist

How to Dental Assit2: Be Productive, Not Wasteful

Let Me Have A Dollar's Worth

Living for the NOW of God

Lose My Location https://a.co/d/crD6mV9

Man Safari, *The* (mini book from Wilderness Romance)

Marriage Ed. Rules of Engagement & Marriage

Made Perfect in Love

Motherboard (The)- soul prosperity series

Plantation Souls

Power Money: Nine Times the Tithe

The Power of Wealth *(forthcoming)*

The Robe: The Lessons of Joseph, Part 1 & 2

https://a.co/d/9Z7COyy

https://a.co/d/gGGB9Rg

Rules of Engagement & Marriage

Seasons of Grief

Seasons of War

Sift You Like Wheat

Soul Prosperity soul prosperity series 3

https://a.co/d/5p8YvCN

Souls Captivity soul prosperity series 2

The Spirit of Poverty

This Is NOT That: How to Keep Demons from Coming At You

Throne of Grace: Courtroom Prayer

Time Is of the Essence

Too Many Wives: *Why You Have Lady Problems*

Tormenting Spirits   https://a.co/d/dAogEJf

Triangular Power *(series)*

> Powers Above

> SUNBLOCK

> Do Not Swear by the Moon

> STARSTRUCK

Uncontested Doom

Upgrade: How to Get Out of Survival Mode

> Toxic Souls (Book 2 of series)

> Legacy (Book 3 of series)

Warfare Prayer Against Beauty Curses

Warfare Prayer Against Poverty

What Have You to Declare?

When the Devourer is Rebuked

The Wilderness Romance *(series)*

- *The Social Wilderness*
- *The Sexual Wilderness*
- *The Spiritual Wilderness*

www.ingramcontent.com/pod-product-compliance
Lightning Source LLC
Chambersburg PA
CBHW062003040426
42447CB00010B/1889